Yesterday and Today

Toys at Playtime

Fiona Macdonald

W
FRANKLIN WATTS
NEW YORK • LONDON • SYDNEY

First published in 1998 by
Franklin Watts
96 Leonard Street
London EC2A 4XD

This edition published 2000

Franklin Watts Australia
14 Mars Road
Lane Cove
NSW 2006 Australia

Editor: Helen Lanz
Art Director: Robert Walster
Designer: Andrew Stagg
Consultant: Susan Gardner, Museum of Childhood, Edinburgh

ISBN 0 7496 3085 X (hbk)
0 7496 3778 1 (pbk)

Dewey Decimal Classification Number: 745.592

Printed in Malaysia

Picture Credits
Cover: Main picture (Getty Images); bottom left (Robert Opie); Bubbles (Geoff du Feu): Interior: Bubbles pp. 6t (Geoff du Feu), 18b (Jennie Woodcock); Co-op Archive p. 7 Lupe Cunha p. 24t; Mary Evans Picture Library/ Barry Norman Collection pp. 9, 15r, 16; Eye Ubiquitous p. 19b (Bennett Dean); Getty Images pp. 4, 11t, 12t, 12b, 18t, 21t, 24b, 25, 29t; Sally and Richard Greenhill p. 27t; Jill Grey Collection/ P. Millard pp. 10l; IQ Builders/Babb PR p. 28b; The LEGO Group p. 23t; Meccano Toys Ltd. p. 22t; Museum of Childhood, Edinburgh p. 13; Robert Opie Collection pp. 3, 6b, 8b, 10r, 11b, 14b, 15l, 17t, 19t, 20t, 20b, 22b, 26, 28t, 29b; Rex Features pp. 14t, 21b, 23b; TM and (c) 1997 Saban Entertainment, Inc. & Saban Entertainment N.V. All rights reserved. p. 17b; VTech/Babb PR pp. 8t, 27b

CONTENTS

Introduction

Today, there are lots of new toys each year.

New toys are made in many different colours, shapes and sizes.

Toys today are bright and colourful. Many move, some even make noises!

These toys were made around 1900.

TIME LINE

In the past, there were not many new toys to choose from. The sort of toys that you could buy did not change much from year to year.

These toys were made in the 1950s. They are almost the same as those from the 1900s (left).

This book will tell you what toys were like long ago.

Look at this time line. It will tell you when the photographs showing the past were taken.

1950s 1960s 1970s 1980s 1990s 2000s

Moving pictures

Today, we watch moving pictures on television and videos. We see moving pictures in films when we go to the cinema. There are moving pictures in many computer games.

It is fun to play computer games. Some games have pictures that move very fast.

This toy is called a *zoetrope*. It was made over 100 years ago. Children spun the barrel round and round and the pictures seemed to move.

TIME LINE

1900s 1910s 1920s 1930s 1940s

Children gathered in the street, even in winter, to watch a *Punch and Judy* show, 1905.

In the past, there were no televisions, videos or computers, but children still liked to watch moving pictures. Some children played with toys called zoetropes, others watched Punch and Judy puppet shows.

1950s 1960s 1970s 1980s 1990s 2000s

Toys for everyone

In the past, most parents could not afford to buy expensive toys for their children.

They bought their children cheap, simple toys, such as skipping ropes, wooden hoops or spinning tops.

This skipping rope is a copy of one made in about 1900.

A wooden spinning top from around 1900.

TIME LINE

1910s 1920s 1930s 1940s

Children playing with wooden hoops, 1908.

Parents also bought little metal toys that cost just one penny each. These were called penny toys.

This toy car cost one penny in 1900. It is made of tin.

Playroom toys

In the past, rich families had playrooms for their children. These were full of beautiful toys.

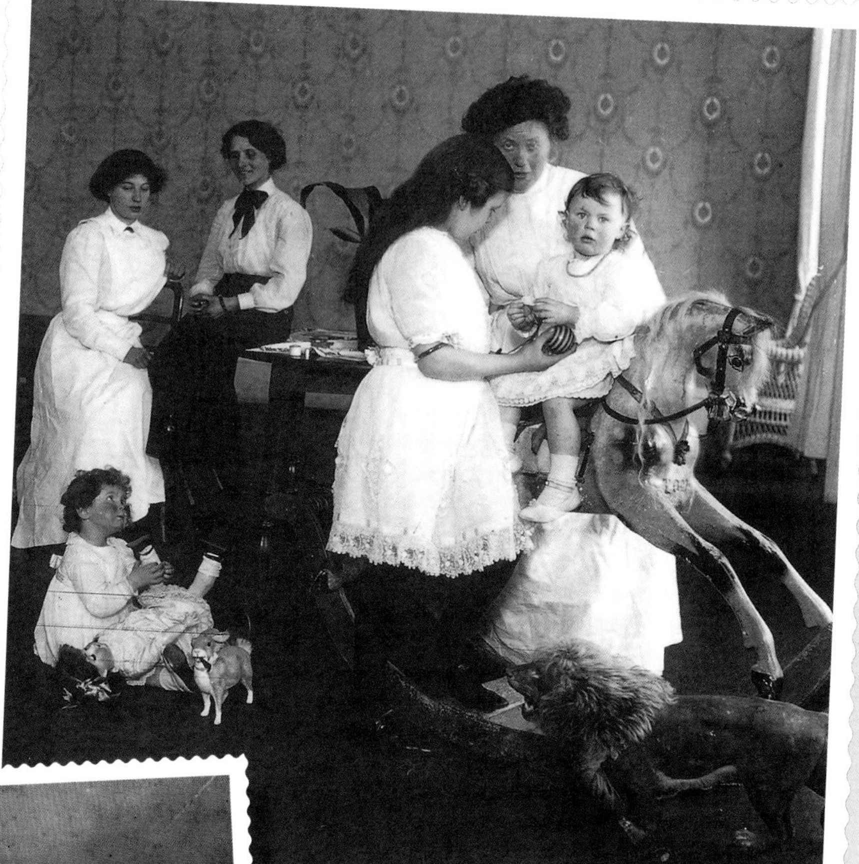

(Right) A playroom in 1913. Can you see the rocking-horse, the big doll and the toy lion?

(Left) This boy was photographed in his playroom around 1910. He is playing with a set of hand-carved wooden animals.

TIME LINE

1900s 1910s 1920s 1930s 1940s

A dolls' house from around 1910.

Dolls' houses were popular but expensive toys. Inside there were tiny dolls and lots of tiny tables and chairs.

Dolls

Dolls have been favourite toys for hundreds of years.

Today, most dolls are made of **plastic**. They have **nylon** hair and wear the latest **fashionable** clothes.

These plastic dolls were made in the 1990s.

In the past, some dolls were made of cloth or **china** (clay). Others were made of wood.

A rag (cloth) doll from around 1920.

TIME LINE

1900s 1910s **1920s** 1930s 1940s

Children with their baby doll in
its splendid pram, around 1920.

This doll from the 1920s has
a cloth face and a cloth body.

1950s 1960s 1970s 1980s 1990s 2000s

Action toys

In the past, children played with toy soldiers made of metal. The soldiers were beautifully made and brightly painted. But the paint soon rubbed off, and the soldiers broke very easily.

This photograph, taken in the 1920s, shows a sister (left) and her brother playing with their toy soldiers and toy *fort*.

TIME LINE

1900s 1910s **1920s** 1930s 1940s

Toy soldiers on horseback, made of painted metal around 1920. Children could collect different sets to make up an army.

Today, war toys are bigger and stronger. Some look like real soldiers; others look like warriors from space.

This plastic space warrior was made in the 1990s.

1950s 1960s 1970s 1980s 1990s 2000s

Toys that move

(Above) A toy plane from the 1930s. It was moved by pedalling. (Right) This toy car from the 1990s is also moved along by the feet.

It is fun to play with toys that move, such as toy trains, cars and planes.

TIME LINE

1900s 1910s 1920s **1930s** 1940s

In the past, many toys were powered by **clockwork** or by springs.

Today, most toys that move are powered by batteries or radio. Some have computer **microchips** inside.

Sparky Robot, from the 1930s, is powered by clockwork. He has to be wound up with a key to make him move.

Remote-controlled toys are moved by radio signals that switch on batteries inside the toy.

1950s 1960s 1970s 1980s 1990s 2000s

Bears and other animals

In the past, children played with toy animals made of clay or carved from wood. Some cuddly toy animals were made out of wool.

A wooden rabbit made around 1940.

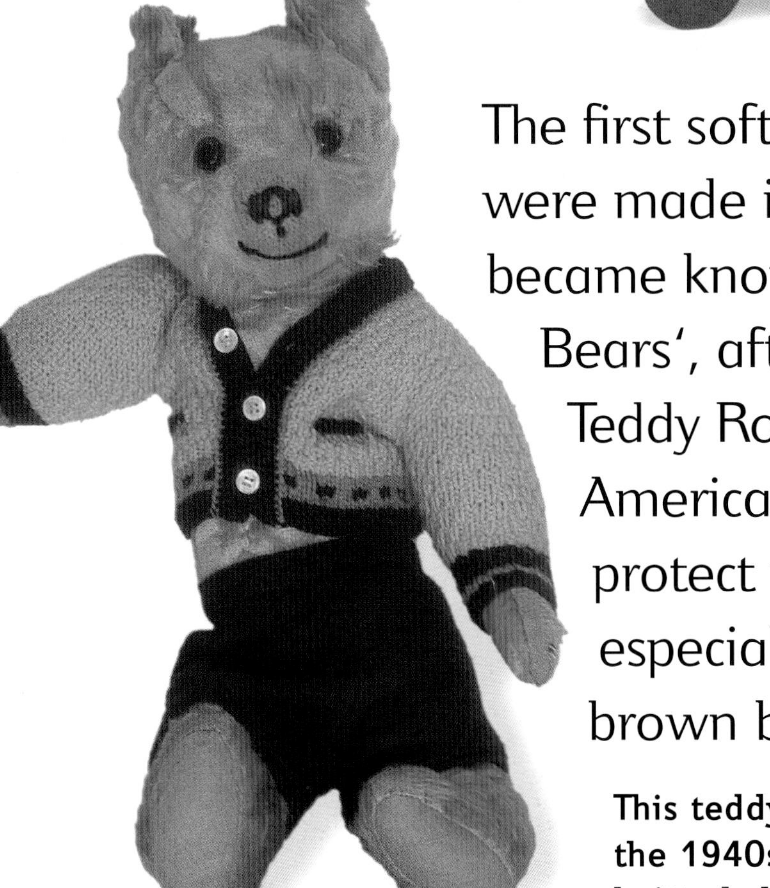

The first soft toy bears were made in 1903. They became known as 'Teddy Bears', after President Teddy Roosevelt of America. He wanted to protect wild animals, especially American brown bears.

This teddy bear was made in the 1940s. He is wearing knitted shorts and a jacket.

TIME LINE

1900s 1910s 1920s 1930s **1940s**

This girl was photographed around 1940 with a teddy bear that is almost as big as she is!

Modern toy animals come in many shapes and sizes. But they are all very cuddly!

1950s 1960s 1970s 1980s 1990s 2000s

Making models

In the past, children made models using wooden bricks. Later, other model kits were invented.

(Above)
A Meccano model from the 1990s.

(Left)
A Meccano model kit from the 1950s. Screws and spanners were included.

Meccano has lots of strips of metal that fit together with screws to make many different models.

TIME LINE

LEGO bricks are bright and colourful plastic bricks that fit together to make models.

They have been very popular since the 1950s.

(Above) A town made from LEGO bricks in the 1950s.

(Left) Models made of LEGO bricks can be simple or difficult. Some models can move!

1950s 1960s 1970s 1980s 1990s 2000s

Parks and playgrounds

Today, most playgrounds have swings, slides and climbing frames. The ground around the slides and swings is covered with something soft, such as rubber, to make it safer if children fall.

(Above) A playground in the 1990s. Can you see the rubber covering the ground under the slide?

This playground in the 1950s does not have special covering under the roundabout or slide.

TIME LINE

In the past, there were not as many safety rules as there are today. **Playground equipment** was much simpler. But children still had a lot of fun!

Children playing on a giant swing in the 1950s.

Foam rubber or plastic

In the 1950s and 1960s, scientists developed many new materials, such as plastic, nylon and foam rubber. They were **lightweight**, bendy and stretchy.

Soon, these new materials were used to make toys.

This bendy toy was made around 1960. It is made of foam rubber and has wires inside.

The wires allowed the toy to bend into different positions, but this could be dangerous. Sometimes the wires broke through the foam rubber.

TIME LINE

Plastic space hoppers were very popular in the 1960s. It was fun to bounce around the playground or garden!

Today, many toys are made of brightly coloured plastic.

1950s **1960s** 1970s 1980s 1990s 2000s

Useful words

china: clay that is baked to make it go hard so that it can be made into things like plates and cups. In the past, it was also used to make dolls' faces.

clockwork: machinery made of wire springs and metal wheels. You use a key to wind it and set it going.

fashionable: when something is in the latest, most up-to-date style.

fort: a strong building, like a little castle, where soldiers live in wartime.

microchip: tiny pieces of a special material called 'silicon'. They form a computer's 'brain'.

nylon: a man-made thread made in factories. Nylon is smooth, shiny and very strong.

plastic: a man-made material that is used to make many objects, including a lot of toys.

playground equipment: toys, like slides, swings and climbing frames, in parks and playgrounds.

Punch and Judy: a noisy puppet play, starring puppets Mr Punch and his wife, Judy. Punch and Judy shows have been popular for hundreds of years.

remote control: when something is controlled from a distance, usually by invisible radio signals.

zoetrope: a toy made in the late 1800s. A strip of pictures was put in the barrel of the zoetrope (see page 8). When the barrel spun round, it looked as though the pictures moved.

Index